Scorpionic Sun

Recent Cleveland State University Poetry Center publications:

Poetry
The Hartford Book by Samuel Amadon
The Grief Performance by Emily Kendal Frey
My Fault by Leora Fridman
Orient by Nicholas Gulig
Stop Wanting by Lizzie Harris
Vow by Rebecca Hazelton
Age of Glass by Anna Maria Hong
The Tulip-Flame by Chloe Honum
Render / An Apocalypse by Rebecca Gayle Howell
A Boot's a Boot by Lesle Lewis
In One Form to Find Another by Jane Lewty
50 Water Dreams by Siwar Masannat
daughterrarium by Sheila McMullin
The Bees Make Money in the Lion by Lo Kwa Mei-en
Residuum by Martin Rock
Festival by Broc Rossell
The Firestorm by Zach Savich
Mother Was a Tragic Girl by Sandra Simonds
I Live in a Hut by S.E. Smith
Bottle the Bottles the Bottles the Bottles by Lee Upton
Adventures in the Lost Interiors of America by William D. Waltz
Uncanny Valley by Jon Woodward
You Are Not Dead by Wendy Xu

Essays
I Liked You Better Before I Knew You So Well by James Allen Hall
A Bestiary by Lily Hoang
The Leftovers by Shaelyn Smith

Translation
I Burned at the Feast: Selected Poems of Arseny Tarkovsky translated by Philip Metres and
    Dimitri Psurtsev

For a complete list of titles visit www.csupoetrycenter.com

Scorpionic Sun

Mohammed Khaïr-Eddine
Translated by Conor Bracken

Cleveland State University Poetry Center
Cleveland, Ohio

Text © Editions Gallimard, Paris, 2009

English translation copyright © Conor Bracken, 2019

ISBN: 978-1-880834-38-1

First edition

23   22   21   20   19   5   4   3   2   1

This book is published by the Cleveland State University Poetry Center,
2121 Euclid Avenue, Cleveland, Ohio 44115-2214
www.csupoetrycenter.com and is distributed by
SPD / Small Press Distribution, Inc. www.spdbooks.org.

Cover design: Amy Freels
Scorpionic Sun was designed and typeset by Amy Freels in Adobe Garamond Pro.

A catalog record for this title is available from the Library of Congress.

Contents

Foreword:
Mohammed Khaïr-Eddine's Moxie

It has traveled with me since Mohammed Khaïr-Eddine gave it to me when we were briefly roommates in Shakespeare & Co., George Whitman's Paris bookshop, in 1966: NAUSEE NOIRE, his very first chapbook (projective pamphlet, may be a more accurate description)—with title in black all-caps on a narrow white field set into an otherwise black cover—published in 1964 in the UK (double exile already!) by our common friend, the poet Claude Royet-Journoud.

It is also the poem that opens the present collection, a translation of *Soleil arachnide*, the 2009 edition of MKE's first major poetry collection. In the first edition, published by Le Seuil in 1969, "Nausée noire" had been pushed back toward the end of the book. It is good that Jean-Paul Michel reorganized the poems for the 2009 edition in their order of composition as this allows us to witness MKE's development with more accuracy.

The fifth line of "Nausée noire" starts with the adjective "intense," which, rereading the poem now, stops me immediately, because it is such a central description of both MKE & his work. In a memoir I wrote after his death & that starts with remembering our first meeting, I say: "What has remained with me from that moment on through all subsequent meetings with Mohammed Khaïr-Eddine can be summed up in one word: intensity. A fierce intensity or an intense fierceness—it was often impossible to decide which it was. Here was someone totally gathered around, or rather, *in* a single point of focus, from inside out: a solar intensity radiating from somewhere deep inside, or better, gathering from *everywhere* inside (soul and skin, organs and bones, mind and blood) to radiate out through a gaze that concentrated the black sun of the interior, twin to the desert sun of his birth place. Black suns, may be more accurate, or as he put it in an early poem: 'My black blood contains a thousand suns.'"

I was startled, then, when reading into Conor Bracken's translation, to find the French word "intense" not translated by its obvious English homonymic heterophone "intense" but by "moxie." Being startled & therefore made to think when you read a translation is always a good thing, I would argue—because the worst that can happen to a text is that translated into another language it sounds, as NTBR critics like to laud it, "as if it was written in English"—i.e., it can be read in blissful oblivion and ignorance of its origin. Translation, Paul Celan said, is "Fergendienst," ferryman's labor, you ferry something over to another shore, another language—& that labor of difference needs to remain visible/audible. The word "moxie," with its various meanings of "force of character, determination, nerve," brings the text into a specific American domain in a way that "intense" wouldn't have by leaving the meaning in a more generalized Latinate language sphere.

The slight *Entfremdung* (voluntarily or jocularly introducing a foreign word to create more ostranenie, i.e., linguistic alienation) has a double movement. First, it locates the "target" language in a specific incarnation—American English—which makes us think back & wonder what the original was: French, yes, but maybe not a plain standard Frenchman's French—& thus we are led back to look at MKE's relation to that colonial imposition that was "French." Second, "moxie" is not a high literary term, but comes rather from an oral popular cultural base—which again allows us to reflect on the fact that MKE himself comes from a culture in which the spoken word is as potent & essential as the written.

It is important to consider MKE's own relationship to his language(s), a relationship nearly always taken for granted in the West, where the natural, the only possible language for the poet is consciously & unconsciously seen as being—as having to be!—the mother-tongue. An exquisite little 1976 essay called "Asinus, asnous, âne" in which Khaïr-Eddine reflects on the Latin, Berber, & French words for "donkey," which he sees as etymologically clearly linked, starts like this: "To write in French is a deliberate choice that was in no way imposed on me. I studied Arabic at the same time as I studied French. My mother-tongue [in French, "langue maternelle," i.e., maternal language], if you can call it a language, is Berber and more precisely, Chleuch (Tashelhayt), the dialect used only by the inhabitants of the South of Morocco."

He goes on to say that "to write in French or in Arabic in the Maghreb is basically the same, in so far as both of those languages are understood by very closed off, and for the most part mutually antagonistic, elites. The Maghrebi spoken language (I don't mean the rural but the urban spoken language) is dialectical Arabic, which has nothing to do with classical Arabic. As long as things will remain thus, there will not be a true popular literature in the Maghreb. This situation is intimately linked to the political evolution, to the liberation or to the enslavement of the Maghrebi peoples." Note that he writes this twenty years after Morocco achieved independence from France, and so the liberation/enslavement binary is not simply a reference to colonial times, but bears on the current repressive systems in the Maghreb.

But, and this is part of MKE's fierce independence in relation to conventional political & cultural constraints, he situates the writer elsewhere even in relation to that which is his most intimate & essential tool—language—& sees him as rooted in a near-ontological estrangement (that word again) not dissimilar to what the American poet Charles Olson means when he translates a line by Heraclitus as saying "Man is estranged from that which is most familiar." Rather than submitting to the given historical conditions, MKE wants the writer to take a stance (another Olsonian word) that shifts his position from one of mutilation to one of conscious outsider-dom:

> The attitude of certain maghrebi authors in relation to the french language is the attitude of mutilated men. This is a grave error, as we know that the writer stands outside of language: he is only a manifestation of History. The true writer is always a stranger to the language in which he expresses himself.

And to make sure his point is brought home, he insists that against the traditional view of the good writer as someone who is in possession of, & thus controls, his language, it is the other way around: "It is [language] that possesses him. In truth, he is its slave. He has to take responsibility for it completely, outside of any nationality, and consider himself as a free writer."

*

From the start I located MKE in a constellation of poet-workers in the French language that lit & linked my night sky across the Atlantic: two in France itself (though both fierce travelers through much of their lives), Antonin Artaud & Henri Michaux, & two on the western edge of the Atlantic: Aimé Césaire & Edouard Glissant. Those writers (at this point much better known in the US than MKE, although all five are of the same caliber) can be useful to the reader coming newly to this book in numerous ways, from Artaud's intense fierceness, not to say metaphysical violence, in works such as *To Be Done with the Judgment of God*, to Edouard Glissant's demand for a "right to opacity that is not enclosure within an impenetrable autarchy but subsistence within an irreducible singularity."

It is too easy to quickly attribute the opacity—or to try to shed a shoddy light on it—of MKE's writing to its being a late continuation of traditional French surrealism. This evacuates the telluric (to use a term close to the work of both Artaud & Césaire) force & the psychosexual attraction & binding energy of the atoms constellating his image-molecules. Nor does it do to tame them or keep them at bay inside a cage called orientalist aesthetics. The Maghrebi & Berber cultural substratum has an autochthonous "surrealistic" ground and a spiritual structure specific to it. The Algerian poet Habib Tengour speaks well to this, suggesting that a form of visionary surrealism has been a traditional, omnipresent aspect of the culture, reaching as far back as the great Sufi sheikh & poet Ibn Arabi to make his point. In the essay "Maghrebi Surrealism," Tengour writes: "It is, finally, in Maghrebi Sufism that surrealist subversion inserts itself: 'pure psychic automatism,' '*amour fou*,' revolt, unexpected encounters, etc.…. There always resides a spark of un(?) conscious Sufism in those Maghrebi writers who are not simply smart operators—go reread Kateb [Yacine] or Khaïr-Eddine."

Go read Mohammed Khaïr-Eddine, now that we are lucky enough to have the volume that opens his oeuvre finally available in English.

Pierre Joris
2019

Black Nausea

I.

An open prism set among the thistle's whims
                                        and no
reason at all to live
                save that I go blindly albeit with more
moxie than all these grasshoppers
                                        their noiselessness
nearly uninterrupted
                        at every corner a new historical marker
the streets crossing me
                        a snag
                                are we fishing again
and caught in the reeds
                                no
                                        the posters lie
see their colors
                        I'll start again at zero if I
have to
                see how this window opens on me
                                        me opening
completely onto a wasteland

II.

this morning the sun is ripe
                     and I'm certain winter
is over
       forgotten the leaden drowsiness
                     the silos bobbing in shadow
where no dreams entered
                     my life ironed like a crisply folded
shirt
       my life washed by its shuddering dread of
becoming
       this morning the sun flays on the window
                                 never before seen
greenish golds
           and falling into my palms the figs
of barbarism
           as into a gap in the rocks it's said were once inhabited

III.

he would plummet from the highest peak
                                    he'd scatter
                                        like
a swarm of gale-slapped bees
                                    leave me alone
with my risks
                    my sorrows
                                my scars
                                    I barely want
to brush you
                    because we are inseparable
                                                every day
facts
            and burning chains
                        which are really men
who strike fresh poses
                                in front of a people
whose sores are eating them
                                    somewhere the blind
                                            hollow
guts
            cities dead in the estuary
                                        will you make it
                                            you're trembling
as the fruit grows nearer
                    a chimney divides the inferno
                                            your sweat

burns with resin and fire

                                        stay habitable
                                              stay ineffable

laughter like sharp gravel

                                      and terror within your

body like India ink

                          it's time for us to go

IV.

my black blood deeper in the earth and in the flesh
of the people
ready for battle
               my black blood harbors a thousand suns
                                  the tragic field
in which the sky rolls up
                  I don't want one more dead color
                                   not one
more sentence wriggling through terrorized hearts
                            you are caught
between me and my black blood
                     guilty of murders worked
traitorously in some dark phase
                 my past pulls itself up too
                      up to my
height
       as thunderous
        as the day that reappears
                            streaming
with black ink
       my black blood
       on a hill
I will drag you through my black-blood-made-mud
       you and me
       former bearers of myths
       my black blood was the ardent milk in the desert's
                                   breasts

you and me
like an implacable wind
                    tons of sand
                                eternities
of molecules
            divide us now
                        because I am the black blood of a
land and a people on whom you walk
                                    it is time
time for the river to groan for having carried too much
                                    like a snake
black and cracking boulders and cedars
                                at the edge of the sea that understands it
                                            standing
                                            present
                                            together
you facing the corpses that weigh down my past
                                        the corpses
worms have not yet desiccated
                            I am judge for having been victim
my black blood runs in the land and in the sanctum of
                                        the people
                                    sole witnesses
and my past lurching out of the lead that shattered it

V.

                              you are dying
                                        but I'll go
with you through the dust you crawl through
                                   we won't reach
the fruit our attention ripens to bursting
                                   we will fall at the foot
of the tree
           where we'll offer ourselves
                              because nothing will be offered to us
                                        you are dying
but I know you as a vernal carcass
                              where the fruit fattens
in the warm hand
                   of whoever will plant you in the midst of the tide
                                                            we
will offer the future's clearest fruit
                              since only we crawl
toward the tree that denies us
                         since under its bark we have found
the secret path each branch ignores
                              you are dying
                                        but I am
naked in the ravenous grass which thins me
                                   and sharpens us together
                                   washes us with stones
we crawl unanimous toward the tree that sways
                              to receive the last

drop of your black blood

                       and to offer to the future this weird

fruit

           which speaks in the mouths

                              of the thousands of innocents dead

in our black blood

VI.

somewhere in my heart
              a dog barks
                                    its tongue eager to harass
those who remove from me my life
                        those who love drinking gallons of
my black blood
a dog wants to sniff out the jackals who tear
                                  with their teeth
to pieces
my life
        my camel life lost in its flight through the desert
                                  where my black blood
its milk
        my ancestors
                        vanish
eyes popped and white as vanished milk a dog runs
a dog no longer seeing print or path
and yet the street rises up to the window
                              bearing again a misery
                                        from which
I make from which you make
                    the unique conviction
                              the camel has lost its
milk in the desert
              maybe it ran under the sand like
the Draa

maybe it filled with my sorrows the sea
a black blood
that was milk

VII.

syllable by syllable I build my name

                                  yours is a long

undecipherable rosary

                  however it is names that leave

like bullets

        that leave stains on the atmosphere

                              it

is names that throw into relief

                names that cut the world

in two

        my name is not an effect of the temperature

                              more like anti-

nature

        I gather shocks

                I pull photocopies out of my reality

see this insinuation

                would I be amputated of a word

                                if I didn't

hurtle into the asphyxia of hours

                bees cold but red

as elytrons unleashing quakes through space

                        they wait

for me elsewhere

        but I prefer to circulate alone

                            thus I incorporate myself

into my bloody multitude

I moonland on an earth of humid indifference
an earth guilty of providing the solemn image of man
let me create a cyclops for the tabloids

my bedroom is

a birdcage
my electronic heart plugged into my gruesome

death
I would rather moonland on an earth that can pronounce
my primitive name
my rival

VIII.

a volley was enough to get it going

                                            ask

the robots

       the sphinxes

              the crickets even

                         they know how to showcase

night

       sometimes a poem will hit me like a stone

                             I tolerate nothing

I am no legend

         that word means to turn against oneself

to end in a sleep from which butterflies are born

                     I've had enough

of powder

       call me he who tempts or deranges

                      in other words

the unwelcome

       but enormous conviction

IX.

                                        o poet you're losing yourself
while the blood of the world
                        is sifted
                                wounded
                        like the soldier
from 1941 who knocks against my memory
                                        and finds no exit larger
than my life
                        opening onto disorder
                                        in the country this year the figs
ripen while the boulder
                        bleeds
                        but see how the room is no
longer enough
                        poet it's you
                                you're feeding with a nostalgia
for the future

X.

I will not describe a bird that collapses

catches fire

have I ever traveled beyond a meadow's promise

and

no hands outside their living bodies

no flesh that does not know

how to locate my center

I will patrol the coastline

won't settle

any tithe that assumes my sorrow

a grim day moves faster than

its noise

and my shadow always like an oil stain

my deaths

I have seen them

lived them even

let them reinvent the stones

shake

the earth

if they leave don't say what the sentries say

they

don't hoist up their present

or give birth to phantoms

because they

walk back and forth

twisting the night

so as to snap the cables of a ship

ready to round   the cape of my life

XI.

death
        eager hyena
                I will reclaim
and proclaim you
            so I can disinter my futile doubts
                        don't I have to
beat or
        brain you
            your nonchalance repels me
                  hyena death well known
are the idioms that made me
               I know how to chisel you
                     I etch your profile
black hyena
        of death
            but how will I expel you
                   when I can't re-
patriate you
      me   stateless
            unroofed
             death
                foul hyena
                  I will vomit all
of you out
      will render you rancid unto your uncertainties
               you were once all embers
and the sand burst like a fistful of salt
           I had to bend

to your angers
        death I was innocent then
                air desired me
                        I was my
own ancestor
        death
            hyena heavy with amulets
                            there is a hurricane
tidying the sahara
          above your angers
                  we stand at attention
ready for a strange fight
            death
            cadaver seeking others
where did I inherit you from
            limp
                coward
                    the world its
                        stasis
                            death
it refuses you
          limp
              coward
                death you can't even enter
a landscape
        it flees
            death not even vegetal
you will never master humanity
        nor the incandescent gold that runs through your rotted
breasts
        death
            grim hyena
                  I will vomit all of you out

XII.

I plotted against my memory
                      it's possible I might find it wrung open
and rusty
        in a thief's pocket
                  I will unstick myself from his paw
I'll follow this lone child who will never go home
                        fashion death
from dried lizards
        one day I will invade the eye that harbors the sea
        but not the fluent mixture
        driving me to distraction
                I emerge brief
                      my
forehead stretched to bubbling
             make images in the arterial phrase where
water rolls around everything
        I scrape the scales off my fever
             and white with murders
explain myself with sextants and jaws
             if I sit outside
my skin
        it's so I can see myself
        allow me to uncountry myself
insurge against myself
        broken
        one cites the numbers

                                        I proliferate inside the egg
                                        roll
stanch
        the cloudburst anointed me gardener
                                        elsewhere I install a gaping
clarity
        elsewhere knock against drowsiness
                                        sleep nude in a pane of glass
the hangover suspends me
                        here is where I end
                                        a king standing
on tiptoe
        wiping down the tables
                        spitting an apocalypse for fear of strangulation
a toad blind at least
                I walk inside my heart
                                        pop it
like a chancre

XIII.

a woman appears in one of my ribs
                                        which a
smuggler brought back from the desert
                        don't worry
                                                never
                        ever have I
been further than my shadow
                        I vomited my clichés into the mouth
of a whore
            near the clear village where your hips are staying
                                        I mean
the lone rock where I found childhood skinned to death
                                    and the wind
cancelled
                close
                            its spinal cord displayed in the hall of fossils
where every day each man discovers his model
                                a thick page blocks me
far from my word
caterpillar which eats me
in the fields where I seem hard to follow
                                        there I am
                        large as your
image
blurry as the graveyard that won't dare contain all of you
                                        expels you

from its schists and anthropophagous plants

                                       because you tore yourself

out of me like a coarse hair

                          and blood ran over my memory
                          freeing the bird that screeched to me your death

XIV.

transformed into icy night
                              unforgettable
                                        I flow
                                        fluid between these
                                        stones
where the day bristles
            and softly mewls from the bottom of centuries
a feral cat
        crow
                    crab
            then the bony saws that prepare my
hostile architecture
                        outside my contents
                                        I am a shrimp and
my stars ooze into tense paths
                        above the hiatus in which cities
corpulent with the rich embed themselves
                                    the corpses
gaunt and strong keep pouring into them their agonies
                            a sea sick
and green with liquid realities
                        blood matters to me now that every
eye bursts
        knot of images
                    eye guilty of creating out of shock
                                    the word
electron that leaps from algae to algae

                                        purging the waterways
of blood that wants to drag heaven to the fingertips
                                        of a peasant
not even hailstorms
                        or ruined fig trees could unmake
here flows the breath of airy tumors
                        myself included
                                        everything has stopped
chewing

XV.

here then are the most unexpected crucifixions

                    and the other

who returns from a burial

              no longer knowing how to respond to
              questions

or how to walk alone among the cypresses of death

                  it seems difficult

to remove this from him

         he says

            oblivion is being oneself a dry flood

                              he

says I am dying of one thirst and I have lost my tongue

                leave me with him

I'll sit one last time at the edge of his vision

             where your muddled

bodies spasm

       splitting their roots

          on the teeth of the knife

raised over the universe

XVI.

I can no longer abide a struggle that miscarries

                          to die crammed

inside one's own senses is surer

                       because you have destroyed the raw

sentence

        monsters flung from your carapaces

        heavy with infernos

           that I should neither stoke nor extinguish

                                 completely

           elsewhere a seashell that only lets in its own noise

it would be better to chew sky and earth

                     yellow with riots laughing at myself

me   menhir besieged by torrid summer

me   this full roundness

             here now in the grass

my struggle is not the grease of a mule

               nor a dove outshone

by the redness of its feet

             it is the gesture of one who aspires to live with

no eternity but one's own wounds

              and the scratchmarks on the heart

grow legible

        in reclusive times maybe ending in dry veins

no

        the cricket no longer resists

        where will our exile start?

Barbarian

o to be a crow with talons mean enough
to hold on among your qur'ans of miraculous naphtha
among the kuwaits of panegyrics
and stars bad weather cracks open like eggs

o fakirs yes I'm a muslim but then autumn arrives
go on revoke my alphabet my luculent uniforms
I have been ratified by explosions
and sulfur mines caving in in the eardrums of waves

lianas overheard
by the geysers of my blood and amber secrets
of myrrh and slingshots
the pistolwhips of the sun the flagrant blows
of boa's belches
of peril's imbecility
my foam and guano body
my bucking cutthroat
soul
rebukes the street flowering like a scar
with umbilical pollen
this is not the weapon
this nursery of incurable words
that slays me slaps and crucifies me
following a cetacean sleep

I am an Ursa Major ramadan inhaling
a casserole of bitter grubs

but you rooted around in the beriberi swellings
dissected the vast river of rubber nights
my thoughts wore down into cups of clotted blood

I spit my heart out
and my name the fig tree whitened by mosquitos' sight
the inverse of saying stamens
like your flesh chanted out by wounds
o shoddy argan tree of barbarism
I toil
in the wet eggy mess of your pupils
I circle and undo your hennaed smile
wood pigeon with dragonfly wings totting its era
with a beak of gas and hoarded bullets
you sprain red my daybreak
macerated in the alcohol of brawls
with an acrid whiff of awkward reigns
which brings to me the flutes' final mirage
and the fire-hecklers in the wind's tonsure
mustang that leers
at each chest missing its epitaph

o to be and to be of your bloods
to gnaw at that snitch the monsoon

Indictment

once the poem has been fed on the white honey of tarantulas
and the albumen of a terrible star
hopelessly exploding under the ash my appetites pump out
once the berbers according to each fantasia
hurl their calabashes into the void of rifles
a conspiracy of eagles hatched by the real cipher
of gratitude and of joy
will sign my fever humid as April
and milky with almonds and floods

once the widowers have stirred the minaret's gray heart
once the children have kissed the scorpion's stinger
then the prose of exile will have soaked enough
for me to sever its umbilical cord with my anguish
and splinter the oars that batter into delirium
the dorsal fin of my exhaustion

o nostalgic little world
let me tuck you in
to the shipwrecking gaze of the living
dead
who read in reports of insidious crimes
the closing arguments of spiders

Horoscope

the wheel of heaven kills so many eagles save you
blue blood
straying through this heart anointed with hyena's brains
simple highways—from the mica leaks a fresh childhood
and skinks my fingers of old nopal
knotted stars and danger in my navels—
old nopal
miscrowned by my routeless dreams of false adulthood
the simoom won't deign to smooth my hatred
because I talk of hypnagogic transmutations
because I brick thunder into the morning's gray wall

cadavers—in the fields of basil where I guzzle
the dirty fluid solutions of geologic fears
the oubliette that prickles under my thumbnail
opens backwards

the wheel of heaven and the cheap virgins
by the fetid bars of the cage of my throat
by my voice turning marshy quietly shouldering
the story of a single pearlescent handle
by the sour milk of endless wandering

I will break you pygmy famines
with a rhythm in which the hands are silent
I will crush
sleeping-stiff-man-silos
you will vomit up our white teeth fouling
the onerous dishes with my blessed blood
of the meager noon out of which heaves my crowded tumulus

land under my tongue
land
like a peasant's reason
silence sawing at the moon's heads tumbling
into my serpentine caresses
and chewing on the black lips of the customs agent
spurted out by a half-bastard of a putrid skink
always friendly though
riffraff of every weather
of your rotting seaweed wraps
of your standards
of your sales on names which still keep
one pure crystal burst of the names
of these squats crowded with the twenty legs
of your humidity
land, exit like a wing

Europe fashions you an asthma of sand
and gutters
Europe
with its fatal rat tail
exit in order to hear winter's final act
no miracle will subdue the wheel of heaven

Memorandum

salvos
and the traffic of black leeches under my retinas—
o sun let your hands dissolve in my blood
inaudible
let me drink you up in one delirious gush

the sky abettor of the witty tips of your uvula
and a slave with frozen eyes who tootles
beautifully on a flute inside my succinct skins
the sirocco's raw vices
make the sun an oafish jester of distress
when my catastrophic jism startles
your lizard pubis
when the wind decrees another faceless insurrection
like a mutiny immemorially awaited
Time's contents
hatch as a centipede inside each eyelid made infamous
by the incandescent estuary
I abjure you—you chap the people's armpits
avoiding the law by climbing inside a quite riotous harpoon
Sun   written into the ledger of my audacities
your pangs stir the folded
curdled patiences
these iguana rings knowing that my palm
still bears the debts of the carob tree
o fearless horses
through the air as if by miracle our souls
stamped with the operative seal are shuddering
each stone summons a childish disaster

I spent last year
rapping on my dromedary hump
and bleeding the placenta of these eclipses
but I never said
I never vomited
the word pistol which does not blink

To White

to white desert—and your trigonocephalic snout ties
delirium
to our sights which have never heard have maybe mesmerized
the shudder of dead lilies and fevers—o hoodlum
limed with blood—over your face I lay a yellow dawn
I daylight the crimes of spring
and the prowling towns gnawing on the wind
whose white sabot violates each moon born by April
the hand to hand measures the abyss where the green woman
hides—and us?
distraught and distressing—while our vacant hands
exterminate the scant beaches in our chests

the wet snout inoculates a delirium of swallows
and step by step our faces object to then delete
the brassline of wasps and shudders—out
of the pothole of spring
nails and plinths turn to face me
but I observe it all from the closed fist of time
while her spangled breasts roll over my face—
a poem
without starting a new paragraph
without me barking
nuptial myriad of white ants
shattering the outrageous balances of rare eclipses
new skin—and sky our teeth
singing out the ounces of ruined centuries
against the face of a flying dog—hello vermin
vermilion virtue—let us dance

on the crests of stars poorly serenaded—this is
making me a turtledove-morning
my mouth of kohl and white iron—which
isn't to say—the rising sap accepts the twists
I give the olive tree of your hips—
we are padlocked cages—are smoke—the place
where streams maroon their sacks of sun

and who crawls into my navel of ocher torrents
and beheads my necks of mesmerized thunder
hips erstwhile laughing
this unangeled sky has found its claws again
but this heap of arcane hemp
loses its way at the base of this wall of cramps
who crawl into my navel of ocher torrents

butcher then my solitary birds
I mean the eye poured into every gram
of bitter amber
smoked and spit onto the advertisement of stars
from which falls my leech-black pygmy voice
go on then butcher my solitary birds

here without commas the threat is announced
by a couple nails I know cut into blessings
chance wants a path
to bivouac here
and the necks of children exalted by the fat sex of rye
and sleep
here without commas the threat is announced

once its fingernails are embedded in the saber's blue flesh
always yelling what weeping who
deceived by obtuse silences drunken moldless night
in which my wife the insect hovers
at least one boat the ocean remembers
once its fingernails are embedded in the saber's blue flesh

files for all the meteors of hallucinated copper
this punic affair strews my debris widely
and unwinds my red wine shadow
with the birdcatcher's female call
but as the sun is a highly spoiled fruit
incontrovertible shadow
this shadow and its wire thread themselves into my skin
files for all the meteors of hallucinated copper

and I am leaving with what remains of me screamed
down as low as the curb
I toast with my glittering defiance sand
beneath the hearty tree where my tornadic snakes
shatter flutes
and I dance my fascination
on the incompetent thorn of your pupils
and I am leaving with what remains of me screamed

I froth with censored poems and absinthe
unerased by a flight of skidding knees
and I insult the mollusk of this conch shell
white in which habit has screwed the bars
which call me surging lion of the unprecedented peacoat
with known audacities from a highly placed swamp
I froth with censored poems and absinthe

now I launch at you the kites of my lungs
in the rigor that wets my space
and I say
spring does not exist it has broken its back
on the wind's deaf edge (palm tree prison
writing to and astonishing yourself)
now I launch at you the kites of my lungs

Mutinies

among other probabilities I need this sea
split like the woman born at the tip of vice
from the fornication of chiggers and yews

shipwrecked
                    how the novice act of my skin
arms   with shouting sea   the red sleep of skins

battered by the complex seal of the stars
I waggle my masts at the blue muzzle of norms

nothing
            but a frightened gulp chartered by the blackness
adjacent to your retinas stiff with djinns—sea
dead by reticules—I close
this thrashing excluded from silence and your whirling
naphtha
by the neighboring texture of the voices of a man walled
into the cracked lips of your orb
and the sun

divided
        I laugh
        sea waterlanding on the unknown ink of birds
by this slash in the sand made by singing
satellites eyes wanderings and midnights

among other probabilities I need this sea
split like the woman born at the tip of crimes
from the fornication of chiggers and vetch

Swashbuckling

white of circles (your lymph bothers my obelisk eyes
but this pond frightens the blue ducks in yours)
and leaning badly on the clouds' teeth
I am the night that denies your privateering
for one last drink of strong moon and trances

my red oil eyes carry you into these circles
flounders burst
bursts the absinthe into yellow mango tree
in your eyes bound to the song of a heaven creeping
among your old earthworm faces

where is the albumen weather I love the weather of shadows cracked
where my mercurochrome frosted-night eyes cry out
the dictated star
that comes alive in the marsupial fingers of music

white of circles (here rolls here the cry no longer soothes)
of tranquil crime of inaudible circles
I am the belt the coffle the thunder
I am the rifle the grenade I am the eagle
and the worm-eaten void of your face from afar

Where

I disrupt the concupiscence of tube worms
where your snowy owl eye consults among white crusts
the venom of my gymnodactyl eye
which bribes the slag of trilobites

where with lovers' leaps and bergs and flux
the spasm of real crickets
reels and sings
—Sagho—my stiff retina accosts my eye

and brusquely melts the forficulids sans pity
for your face ringed by the blue milk of scarabs
and the rye where thunder drops insignias
flagrant with a hysteria as pretty as contumacy

Description of a Flag

for Mehdi Ben Barka

jaundice of lamplight cracking open the dream's plasma
and the rain that roams over me dissolved
into the proper sap of sky and snow
ruffled by a god painted on my cramps
o heavens here they are nude and matted my faith tear dreams
in the classifieds that uncoil the rectum of my land
hung up by the hooves like a sacrificial cow
I delete the slanted notebook of your precision
and raise a coffin made of mint and thyme
o land remembered gently under the ancestral vice
shout wide when we climb to the white stone
our pockets jangling with the most beautiful coins of air

hurry up fresh heads and
this nail bleeding in my eye

death is a leaf of tobacco
you ponder the swamp death is a bold feat

hurry up fresh heads and
this nail that traps my eye

death is a kaleidoscope
in which you interrogate yourself finger and navel
after clasping the wormy void of your flock
of carbuncular birds the day's asbestos
flaming and the night's firing

o hurry up how drunk with combat
on this morning of edible horrors
in the bay of a memory never cherished

your face already locked up
the sun like an almond tree overcome
in a shiver of myriapods
and we were unique among all those
who saw a throne of insects reduced
to the level of the hurrah of an island rising
out of the sea's blood crackling with joy

and now
death
you like a reed whose songs' volume
the scarab picks

jaundice of lamplight cracking open the dream's wisdom
solar disturbance ousted from the barbarian fabric of the post-
reign
which we redden and sign
with the antelope star flying over this day
over this desert psoriasis we've dug ourselves into

suddenly you die and shake your roots at truth
in my improvisatory shadow where moved they ponder you
the men of Saguia el-Hamra sprint
on the chergui the Seine has drawn over you

crawlspaces
lengthen
spider eggs perfuming the authoritarian silence
murder white on the rim of despair

the Bou-Regreg tells us who morseled you and where
your blood laughs again at the public enemy
revenge desiccating the throats
wormy
with the eyes of stones soaked in the boilers
of a life that draws itself closed up high and simple
to damn
no
to harpoon the king that shark who has
left the bed of rivers of polar scrub
and gnaws his grudge sometimes
like glass balls that shatter
jinx soot king
narrowness of dreams
of always sifting the flag of blood
of the song that strides through our viscera

The King

in my stigmata I carry a king who parches
one thousand uvulas roughed up by philandering lightning
assegais hammered on my thuggish star
I carry a king in my vaccines who makes roar
the lion cubs of a childhood divvied up in winter
my apodal legs measure the tepid danger
opened by little puffs of ascomycetes and lilies
I peddle in my lungs an old leper
and his people a scandal of ankles knotted in sprains

the mantis shrimp of childhood weave a bitter memory
in the violet anus of the seas
I carry screaming
black and rutilant and nailed down by an ostentatious sky

how to seize the king's nose
or his assassin's head
between his legendary hands that push their cobras into my head

the real sun limps in the traces of the torrent
of my opprobrious cumin-dusted life
blood strangles me and the king toasts in my left eye
while drinking my right
the king executes me
with his leaden fur and my luxuriant shadow
outside (I throw my crutches
white into my rye fields sweaty with
spiders sculpted on the pump of delirium)

which shows my balaclava of reared-up earth
my greetings of rust inverted
in the files of the pink laurel
of my land which we call the stone-of-the-wind

the king splits my clockface to check in
the era's hydra—the thick-locked crowd
carries its eczema of thunderstorms with more grace than the white
Fridays on the black shore

I carry a barrel of middays king minus my fever
along the curves of a horizon sick with the joy
of thorns
and the milk of figs fallen out of the stars' unrest

like the mayflies incinerated by the outdated labels
of spring
like the scoundrels redeemed by the final jailer
like the double u of the birds of my eyes
trapped in a tear and building caimans
in muddy lengths on my almond-scented nights

your words pink scree
a taste of snake

like your statue remade with my whitewash

I pull the nails from my body too high to be wept over
I give you my blood to burn
your erotic moons explode over my journey
gnawed on by dogs
your throne rolls ruins with attacks on the clouds' helmets
and flogs your hogback at my window

44

I was standing in the center of a cadastral map when he appeared to me yellow and the color draining thinned eventually stretched over his quirks they tell me our love was hoodwinked the Field of Lyres hauled itself over my hooded shoulders I found under a headless jackal the shrewdly tanned skin of Goats I spread it out sat down on it waiting for the requisite dreams death to the king birth to oblivion the prey built its heaven and terminated itself my cheek morphed into the laughable sex of a bee the metro climbed back onto the rain let's recall that I was yelling at the disappeared this sure ain't a daydream because the least of my words is a shiver of your massacres I made them a hall-pass to get them to the frontier of Fact ringing like one drop of crucifixion I was sitting down my legs crossed over the maps of my misfortune.

they lived in the narrow flames of candles ate the legs of roaches drank their sweat invited the asian flu and cancer into their boxy little face they let saw-toothed iron things grow around their ankles and took advantage of my pres-ence to cut their tongues to size we are the land and the king vomits in our sour blood we are swallows in the necessary gust of wind we dare wear a flag of wounds they trundled like old mules through the flour of the Curse and didn't believe my wrinkles my cleverness slapped me my longest arm left me my revolt knocked at the thunder-jawed door I walked the entirety of Paris fifty times and I saw ardent women and greasy men milky girls smiled at me but I could only do good by them by staring attentively how can you love when you carry disaster between your lips at the station café the table's hand grabs by the throat the king who raises my gorge like the stirring of an invincible monster the beer rose in my stomach and after a brief barrage fell back the chicken with the golden eggs on my matchbook responded with eggs of ash and made me drink them the Goats knowing I was vomiting their monarch crept out of every hole in the slums and surrounded me without explanation but they couldn't get close to me I would strangle the king who was already dead in my fingers the old argan tree greeted me a lizard delivered a fraternal telegram from all the reptiles glutted on jujubes and rage millrace of horror and red chains I saw again my village perched on the trident of Time I paddled again through the violet stone of the mountain at night when my bones folded into themselves the blaring of the guerrillas of pink sand the Spaniards danced the seguidilla the Italians put the Holy Spirit on an overheated train and every person in the world swept the highways clean and raised a great ruckus in the manner of the maps of the stars and savannas I lead the world out of the Citadel I hang it from the dialects of miniscule light it rocks with the pockets of a man who falls into them as if from a nest robbed of eggs before the snake makes them jump with his heat the sun drank up all the politics on Earth the king beat himself in a duel with the devil who always shoots first the king is slope Paris is cage the sordid king with his bad posture without clothes the Goats in a Line warn the mangled feet

my apodal legs measure the tepid danger
opened by little puffs of ascomycetes and lilies
I peddle in my lungs an old leper
and his people a scandal of ankles knotted in sprains

with the mares of your early years
with the rapids of Nigeria and the singing flotillas of Ifni
with the marbles of the palace of an altercation in shards
of lizardless lynching
the chief of the abyss diggers
makes you a death sharper than the razors of the waves

from your bracelet of centipedes of Vesuvius in salamanders
from your flat whiffs and Marrakesh's wall of laughter
from the plates you use to eat my coldness and cirrhosis
from your saracen wheat aflower with the flames
of your toga
I come down
pause
I knell the death of the king who dies in my palms
of the king whispering in the claws of the pond

the mangled feet of old oil barons that drag through the pharmacies a halo of unrecognizable countryside and tubercular poetry at the bottom of a flat ditch the body the seed galls attack the shuttle of my blood the seed galls with gloomy faces with avalanches of stars broken on heaven's collar burden of numbers I no longer expect anything else from the fabulous void nor from the turtledoves I was hiding in my wallet THE GRUDGE on bank bills and bus tickets mouth irrevocably shut fingers ready to dive again into a task whose risks the Apple's forgotten I watched them from the seam stared at them I tried to rescue them I weathered midnights white as talc they were tied together by an old pact with deception I rebuffed my disarray for a time but without knowing it I made flies with scrapmeat and chancres I couldn't leave an establishment without difficulty couldn't get up one night they had to use a custommade product to peel me from my chair I lived again through my breathing love graveyard flowers and falls from a great height and little by little I ended up in the Umbilicus where always it's always Night.

you lashed us to the rush that wilted before the flood
you gather us into hypothetical snits
you grant us amnesty and claw our faces with mute reproofs
mute as the water of death
as a gunshot in the heart of my heart
you abduct us

my table remained deserted my family made of
spiders and reptiles invades your desert-dry eyes
and the Mosquito drank the sea in front of the Ramses of your lightning

king rebel
king blizzard of threaded needles and a thread of needles you cover my head
with a swarm of crickets my cries recall
I find you again in one of Hitler's trenches writing out the
account of your cavalcade of onagers and insidious rawness
hailstorm vast and stunning the despair of crumbled dawns

king infantryman
and the red sap throttles the cedar
and the river again dredges up the thirst and hunger
of the woman who gives birth to colic
even a forgotten qur'an wormy dregs in the sluice of my
fugue and the people rub their hips against the hedge
at the foot of your vanity
and I recite the names of baraka and suffering hiding between
the layers of autumn
the names of the source the muezzin finds in a single ounce
without speaking
which you offer to me
I camouflage badly my solitude
the names of the golden laurel
the names of neurasthenic caverns
and because my hair unearths the catastrophe
in the street I spread the pox of your names
scented with drops of nightmoths
but too bad ranuncular weather hauling the swamp
too bad if they cadge the veins from my assassin flab
knowing that to survive the reply is a beach
where the morning leans to recover its health which is
an eagle
and the heads rolled by the knives of my vertebrae
and the drum-circled cities
and the weddings perhaps   thinks the sand
of the men in
my rosette windows and my kohled lashes

while a harbor's hiccup
whistles and plays
my voice

the king of damage in his sarcophagus
from the Umbilicus bent by the eclipse
against the very green outline of my silence
where fantasy listens to the sun
I crush him already an animal

not king
not furor
but this power of a day seismically shucked
sunk
in the black milk of my palm grove

Barrage

horse
     dead
          shifty
               shoals
                    under my fingernails
jackal of the race of big malices
God dies without a sparkle a log in his arms
between my skin and me
                    rises high inside the vine
and the faces
one by one
each one thick
lacquer one pours
over the walls
a thousand prisons
lynchings
kasbahs unearthed by a cyclone
                    here misses the eye
a rigid fist
     I suspend myself from the void
                    and suddenly the nightcrawlers
of childhood
the slithering of green silt
                    gusts
                         I bed down above
                              brusque flood
the lost rose
becomes tongue
then manure

hey hyena

        tonight I drink the forbidden liquors
        right   words
        left   words
        take a seat
              toads all along my
                  spine

the moons fly into stars
        balls
        like folkloric dances
        oh this South between my straight legs
        this mouth exiled from my saliva
        women climb onto the high-wire
        electrons
        butterflies
        dark unalluring veins
        forgotten in some street
        beneath a magical fresco
        where to break is to abolish the law
        ignorance
        retractable sea not
        just city without city
        and human without human
    shadow that collapses in long chapped fissures
a ship will leave the port of my joints
              what a rogue this guy talking about
              setting
              fire
              to the black cat popular
              for the intimate
              mystery of its purring

hold on

quiet down
remember
imbecile
they lend an ax for my language
they oust a king I flatten his riches
I am the black steer you're seeking
fugitive of memories in rubble
     and torture
          even though land is
   no longer land
     stone
      no longer stone
grilled by the cherguis
      swallowed
    just like the dawn that brightens your face
you
  delirious lady
    you
      moaning beast
         me
       acrid standing in the thickness
of my entrails
    shambling
     gnawing on scrap metal
         body in negative
I ruin in rooms
    one throws down their cargo of sins
sweat and heat
   ah
   pustulant gaze
      I seed
        and seed again

                                                    with garbage these
fields
old sabers
cannons
mosquitos
cramps
throughout the retreat of angry stars
                        the gentleman feasts on closets
he ends in an apostrophe
                        smashes into the depths of another gentleman
behind me
at the end of me
                standing on top of me
a satyr has apparently saved himself from a cold book
wrings my neck
me
an ember
                hey hyena
                        drink me up
                dawn will burst in one of my wrinkles
nothing to be done
                they climb back up
                                        crabs
                                        cylinders
                                                smoke
                                                        robes
give me your voice sir
                        I want to hear mine
                                        a lightning bolt
pukes
        a spiral that soon whines
                        all the kids in hell

  the

city
        takes another bite
                    hyena give me your elastics
                                                    and let's drink the dawn
like it's a clone fresh and slow the dawn
right under your nose

Gennevilliers

They got to know each other in Paris between two smoking faces which it was said were fired blanks. The machine guns launched black and yellow texts onto the café terraces. Ancestral huts and migraines crucified the gossiping sun of a late autumn in which convalescents were stretching out electrified limbs. One spoke adroitly about these rhymes bees of inconsistent blondeness. They weren't listening or pretended not to hear. In their navel rooted the reign of a sphecoid wasp-star which itched throughout the discussion. They were anxious to go home however their legs had become the sole emblem of a museum of the nearby desert. They broke their ribs several times in the middle of the terrace. At a neighboring table the devil applied his makeup. At that very moment a tom-tom unleashed a drumbeat inside their stomachs and inexhaustible molecules. In their left lung Zodiac howled; and Time, whom one never meant to interrupt, plummeted incontinent and sat on their sentences, chewing them like birdshit. Time fled past the trashcans. Zodiac partied hard with long and bloody fireflies.

agonies
caves
menstruation
you corner me against the white wall of legends and against
the forced flight of the falcon whose beak accuses the saharan's face
in the midst of a sheep stampede
the girls smelled porphyry exploding from our grottos
the rifle measured the cloud from the riot's fires
and spat
the monstrous name of a chewed-up king
rust and sardines in this desert where prayer
is drinking
the cruel mouth itself

the drum of the sky yelled at every ensign
and the woman still damp with the complicit dawn
with apple trees and treasons
with gray cobras
with maroon business and bursts of woodchips split down
to the trunk
whistled in the strangeness of a throne made out of centipedes

The head of the other had spurted out of the africa on her back.

gentle the myth that spurs me
gentle this traffic of inextricable salts
and this Gale of evils and tongues
my mother never knew handles so rich
in whirlwinds of birds boring into my skin
softly this frozen head and these regurgitated salvos
in the rocky ditch of my life
of my hand tangible and gentle this present century
the straightforward concupiscence of roses and the abyss
in which is scrubbing itself clean
this unfinished people

The voice had attracted gawkers who stood like scorpions ready to strike. But they weren't even watching. They were whipping the cats of delirium. We had dug them a nice grave inside their solemn mucus in which the unerased and not at all affected devil pissed after his protoplasmic orgies. We went door to door. Everyone had the right to one blow of the truncheon. We decreed a cold war ramadan. Salvation went all the way to God the Innumerable thrown into the dusty attic like so many planks and bent nails. We taxed them like spellcasters. They hadn't yanked on the king's tail. We blurred them. They were born again from their bitumen. We barbarized them. But they civilized the incantations and carried high the carcass of the manitous of unincorporated factories and stations. We tried to fool them. They didn't have a coach to rent. We arranged them one behind the other like pouting children. They leapt at the throats of precepts and silenced them. Elsewhere, we tied very tight ties. We waited for the true billboard to finish bagging heaven. Money slit throats in the slums. We confirmed the customs fee was not a toll. We puffed up, scattered brains, ratfinked and clinked drinks. We were blue-yellow-green.

gentle
this vulgar science
gentle for the couscous of your thunder
which vomits in future entrails
gentle this lagoon
gentle parrot
stud farm of renewed sales and paling jaundice
end ending the obstacles
and the abased order of skewed legends
finishes off your ink of roses

The convoy of delirium went farther. We saw shell casings in the brook. What puddle below me?

I am this lair and not your uvula
swayed by the involuntary shudders of coitus
and spare change
here's an asphyxia doubled by sulfuric asthma
and your audience
broken if not crisscrossed
by sluices and debits

The Headquarters was erected in the middle of the slog. A peacock protested this ravenous war. We say LAUGH.

from a grimace
from a flint
from a fire in which your dreams are parapoems
from a prowler
from an acolyte
and from complication over everything
comes the silence in your urns
from a trumpet
arranged in the mad window
and how not to truncate these geometries
I unchain them
from an epileptic
saint
scissors
we want a blank screen
we want a tree beyond ourselves
this season shucks itself and finds our true faces again
and your soapwort heads
vomit-covered muzzles

oh our pricetagged heads our necks without axis
our poppies by these meadows of children
and this rare perverted sweating mosque
the calamitous cricket of curare africas
from a simple game of echoes rising again and billowing
when you detach the iguana's rings
from an afternoon turned toward the moons
of a clairvoyant disorder
of a fig
by this Congo cheated of lymphic stars
of mistaken knocks
of a neverending anguish

we watch you in the irises of an ill laugh
but here are some zigzags a nubile sorcery
king
my gallows nocturne
boo king by the staircase of absence and Evil
and your laughable nettles
which the cyclone of my songbird eyes
that doesn't fear the snares in yours
will soon hurl over the hedges of vice

For My Wife

shouts of whitey and fear and anguish
of the nude night plucked out
of the cold flight of thirsts' dreams—from my steppe
I have the enormous memory of a lion licking
the blue figs of devastation—
where the storm armed with my birth spasms

I hear you under my carcass of bricked blood
bundles of stars puked up by the storms of childhood
of opuntia cactus in which the trionyx and amber circulate
but I carry unhappiness I carry a damnation of olive trees
to the jujubes of births rejected
by the massacre
when through the hybrid fields of eyes you stride
like the moon fallen into the milk of mygalomorphs

Annigator

it is a dream in julid skin it straddles me
holds my shadow rapt it's a flounder an acrid hip
its blood deposits my sirocco body
into ink into a mouth with ash-streaked lips
It is a blast of irreplaceable terror a drilling
bird with
all the leaves that deliriously follow it
into the rapids where thunder dumps our cutting

It is She who tenses me from behind
this shadow of cursory obstacles
and lithobes burrowed into my mind
where with beltsanded stars I debride
the oubliettes of her eyes It is Time
whenever I allow myself a sun-seared night
and words that will shatter your test tubes in a single
specious strike!

He who is about to be born
(I will call him Alexander!)
will have bulletproof skin
and an onyx skull
and a member as miserably beautiful
as the gray rose of cyclones
as the talon of Guevara
he who now is born
will die inside the applause
of a crowd who fornicates
with wall safes.

Sagho

the bloody morning sprinkled the legends born from dregs
from stars deflowered at full speed
and it lifts my blood like a mustang ringed by eagles

from the high plateau where your fingers fold the sumacs' fire
to the steppe cracked open by the beaks of ernes
I beat the sky with the questions of my fists

milky morning salt of lilies and agrotis moths
the abyss rewards us with the belly of an antelope slaughtered
in the thunder's millet

but not a word
not a word if not the flour of lyctus beetles by this masculine weather
and by sheaves the aphids of wind under catnip

too bad so lonely too bad I forge the public flag
of dawn I wipe my eyes with it before entering
the inextricably fair tradition of time

To Jean Dufoir

the atrocious sun of dreams
the sticky cadaver of moons and the desert
when the sea rocked by an intoxication of bitter algae
hyphenates the malleable heavens with your black
gazelle face
there under the boatman's damp armpit
are more of them than birds on all the earth

the sepulchers have fallen into the chilly rivers

a weapon was needed: my dried-up tongue my blind tongue
spitting out the intrepid horses of the flight
of superstitions
and the rites
of a spring disemboweled
by our stiff feet
and here stretched out on my skin is
the slanted dog of aborted threats
heaven lowered
torpedoed raiding our faces
the soured fossils the uniforms
and this sickness on their gray pupils
viaduct
and
silence by the slithering of these numb pangs
but
what is a flower if not the death of tarantulas

I say this black and white or maybe violet fire
among the roofs rotted by distance
I say the airplane-housefly-strange on our viridian necks

and we were wondering if we hadn't been drowned
centuries ago
I say this immanent order this suit of a stillborn eagle
I say nothing let's move on past so few busted handles

the sepulchers have fallen into the chilly rivers

our march was a fine
and docile line
our arms clacked
against the mulish sky's smooth back
and our half-developed eyes
on your faces bloomed among the brambles
when
rejected by the tornado
our bodies swollen with emotion formed
small puddles in the liberty

Laterites

worn out from being nude among the marvels
of a strange and yellow life
where your silence dines with my true birth
on tables that memorialize the sweet and frigid void
      you are the star towing enormous blood by contempt
worn out from being white as the smiles of men
who walk backward down a street where they won't drink
the oaths of the eclipse
or terrible legends
      I leave you now for the illicit eye
      high as the weather halted over my knees
      neither green nor brown
      but
the impregnable laugh out of which ospreys fly
mocks the vast alibi of clouds of sand
whose every grain
my throat gives alms to
the way the natural horizon recedes
further with every word you mix
into laterite alcohol with africas of blood
too beautiful to be the source of the recorded heaven
worn out by your arrays
this is my pipe and tapir snout
      not murder anymore
this is believing that every pond
knows how to lay an egg like the gecko deleting
my double birth
      it is I whom I oppress
      with this not less fractured
      lousy time to be in business with abysses

Scandal

for Aimé Césaire

o echo-toothed negro o my intangible river
listening only to the green of Caribbean syllables
because our ancestor still burns the banana tree
hair straightened to match the archipelago's angles
no foam dies without this erect evil-eyed asp
showing up skinless inside the african bone
or fanning out in bushfires whenever someone
comes out of the bamboo interior
be done with the nostalgia for hours fogged by hatred
the soul offs itself with a blue flail rebounding to center
shouts to death from inside the hyena's pores
as if the sun were the only written thing
can a trap or remorse or no longer being anything matter
if not the nausea of some vanished puddle
if not a newspaper column opened to the bird
derision if I was saying sudden mustang
they still recite monotonously our legends
is this museum so rare and what horror
we don't make God out of dead wood
we have in our fists a thousand sticks of dynamite
o my throat slopes like a well-traveled path
here I am amid the laughing pack hot
with other births where with radiant napes
the fireflies are undrinkable here I am
stem and honey lambasted by a silence
too clear and the guts of the abyss
check out the star how it climbs its centipede

feet my unrevealed spine
is dying my mind is dying I need poetry
not the azure in which cities fuse together
not the lymphatic eclipses
only poetry of the hearts of peoples lain like rugs
under the viridian rubble of my conscience
it is raining again it may be that this time a land
appears hairy under my roasted skin
they are so heavy the lepers of the underground world
poetry my liberty my bread of trembling suns
here I am day after day drawn with different flames
lick your pointed feminine toes gnaw
my poetic flesh unqualifiable fowl
and you monarch go manage my bistros
bash me against the nettles less bold than a mule's language
tear holes into the flock with your teeth drown me
in your shit the color of ancient grappa
but beware I carry the pullovers of a rusty age
the chemistry of audacity has ruined the amber
out of which I was falling like argan trees
killing the circumcised
fly and pluck nude my wing
the cosmogony of a word
to live and to wound
the rival the pillaging mother
who threw you into this nest of carnage
but invisible here you are firm and venomous
sure of them pouring in your eye your black fever
and because the night wanted me to be its water
bathing me in it a man the fingers of love unfeather
and because the boulder was speaking
to the soft and perishable swimmer

who was pulling me against my will
into this intruding water
I arm and remove myself from each of the song's branches
oxygen that uses a surfeit of life to kill

an eddy of rats our sewer our island
underneath your incandescent steps
underneath the dust raised by death's passage
underneath unviolated seasons to which we are
bound by the terrible cactus of being men
in the plural with the claws of those who latch on
and this old view from inside a vagabond's memories
these names given by other chewers of solitude
and these too my photos which hoist soluble dyes
up to the menacing sky that cracks the heavy gate
of a ghetto never opened and these my poppies
shatter the frozen sources of wind in my palms
this the child of planks and nails twisted
like this lode of army ants under your armpits

here's one for us
                    the tarantula coiffed with asthma
lubricates the perfect instants of this summer night
corruptible if it incubates a nothing of a man
wild if it sets trembling in the kneecaps another anger
making and unmaking at the same time but what has this
venom come to make with my joy
                              the other shits in a bush
found in a dream because he's wasted with wafers
the tree had to be made outrageous without hard muscle
but a graph of untenable thoughts
on which sits completely nude humanity

white worms of excrement will make flowers and idols inside them
cortege of products avalanching
from the obtuse summit to the tributaries
the arenas will retain a taste of horseback
and my child's eye I will be able to swallow it
like a pill jagged with screws the absinthe is too bitter
o berber! how to rise up from the filth
make a chain from the hypothetical they place on my back
stone after stone here is the castle of time
Senegal with its marble paths and the slaves
but so much fortune and so much opprobrium
bring me to suicide every day and every morning
Césaire I am an other but only barely
does the sun touch my capillaries
exposing my memory and roots
thick with sunspots and blindness
and they call me citizen king who at every turn
loses his crown
     which is to say slave fallen abruptly
but brother our treasure is first the Caribbean Sea
and the coral that flares in the mouth of the waves
and the pink gilding of the sea and incredulity
all the convulsions of a love steadfast and serene
the real reason to surrender
      hello
       there
        Césaire

Exile

We carry the old rifles of the colonized
we stress our rage until our faces are twisted
against the ardor of nudity against the scorpionic sun
we carry the bomb our single torso swaying
we honor the sawdust of our navels by the harbor
too hard those old hibernian kings OUT OUT

Stiff hide
hide
a tambourine my fear a jackal corralling and wiping the mucus
of the dead
newly recruited into my parricidal administration!

my flute enlists in and finishes
the ambush your rebellion won't pass by
busted island of my friend Césaire a Hun according to Faye (was he wrong?)
An autonomous void according to the stage and a black musically enamored
with neuroses
according to
Sartre
preposterous! A friend descended from psychodermic metal!
ha! the forest eons ago
dead with no pandemonium THE LITTLE METAPHYSICAL TURN!
I throw ferns into the kettled marl I tempest
I light up Africa I spider I mite
my alcoholic snow and my little cup
I find my skin under a derided heaven I slip
between it all
the black.

I set revving
plagues beautiful as your women
in the depths charred by starless asthma
and I lone runt enter among the worst stegomyiae
to where the sea hacks up its blue song which a jackal
disembowels under the arcane anger of your udder

no
longer a dove!
it multiplies it is white it is
standing up
did I say
blood without Bandung
so poorly argued such is fife but when
then will this hydrocarbonic vine explode?
my language stumbles violet over it my isthmus language!

we drag behind us
the childhood of spiders (MUTILATED)
country of exile broken thirst old oaths!
I insurge against myself It spins yarn from the wasps
of the nefariously beautiful black slut-bird
while time grinds gold ingots to dust!

Refusing Burial

I'm not lamenting this taunted blood
but a cast of hawks
high as the blood carries its irremediable bill
with the sluice where death leans into my eye

o sun
your crutches shatter now
the brief cry of earth clods tossed at the heavens

my chest is an arms cache badly shut
and leaps better than a cricket
over the silence of my eye
over the charm of the echoless rock
where the berber laps up his retinas

over your death
André Breton rejected
by the grave to which the eye nailed the sun
by the sole murder by the day toasting
with hemlock poured into your idioms
but since the war in me is a maimed affair
since fantasy is a soap that does not wash me
of the viridian men
who rebel against the dead wave of oceans blooming
into specter
          me the only one surveilled by my gestures
sniped dead by a time worse than the poem
          the real time burns its hair in the red honey
          of our voices

while negation carries this man in its tits
to the highest raid from which purity gushes
liberty is not milk or star or reason
virility police not the joy of a dead season
but this impenetrable blood
under your fingernails
they say death but what is a star without a cavern
a head
if not a target offered to the present sewn up with crime

strange
strange threat!

Each wind carries in it my death perfectly designed but I say to each wind Here's my death and I have mapped myself so well my edges no longer have a place to exist. I hand my death out like shots—in the only street whose end is no more solid than a look rusty with absence and a crappy array. Your death is not just one death one box of matches hanging from the bottom of a bar not a glass of white wine not a clove of agony on the basement parquet where poetry lies pregnant and who wouldn't drool over all of the gold appalled by the solitary individual spectacle of our systematic burials.

O poetry gag me now!

The last word does not exist. The dynamite of the first word is enough.
Men my kegs of powder; men immunized against man;
man you have no more time to doubt;
man you lick your spittle and don't limp backwards;
man lost look;
when poetry ripens into the pure green of delirium and when the
desert has surrendered its water to the incessant evil that fueled you
André Breton

when man has blown out Aladdin's lamp
when Ali Baba has claymored the void
when Jesus has finished devouring his cross
when Mohammed has hoarded enough money
to burst every pipe
the eye turns to me
I sell my death
I am wounded in the chest
—apple tree
old armor
prohibiting neither Eve nor Adam
but the atomic silence that stipulates me
to the millions of stacks of skins I will carry
into the anthology of the incinerated world

But why slaughter oneself to save just one word hollowed out by termites a
house that collapses as soon as one enters

I GREET THIS HORSE FALLEN FROM THE PINNACLE
ANDRE BRETON
FROM WHICH POETRY SPRANG LIKE A SPRITE
POETRY MY MORGUE MY SERENITY AND MY SHIPWRECK

Scorpionic Sun

sun contused by test tubes
enter the simple hieroglyph of scorpions

the flies look at
my occiput where packed in with feces the sun
fashions a disaster out of the shrieking land of our cadavers
old counterfeiter
I scrub crudless a poet fallen into his retinas
a poet who doesn't tell the moons
his name riddled with ditches jealous of stars
and which catalogs the thaw's green teeth
myriad whelk protoplasm sextant resin
where the eye sacrifices the indicted legend
to the carcasses of myriapods poorly locked
so prudently by the grudges' gapes
the earworms enumerate my urge
bicycle trapdoor skip-a-beat heart such an old block
of bagged seniorities and futures returning
via the grimaces of the old provider of word-caverns
the scales-of-memory have split open like elytrons
the steel mill flawed
by the spawn of birds braying for a zither
by gold beaten into a simulacrum of wings
where the baffling lack of involucres thrashes

frenzy splendor alcohol eclipse
this trench that doesn't answer
for the wars donated by my memory
forgotten by saints broken and cross-eyed
over this heaven fallen

around me   he
onto whom the tribe throws its vermin

Noon in the city. Factions, blowguns, potions. Children heave barrels onto carts. Scandal dragged into the light. The Weapon gets me. I am sitting on a heap of newspaper and misunderstood dreams. I swarm: hemipters. Not spring, not summer. Sleep and dead birds, attacks on an unacceptable fantasy. I smoke keef and heaven. The stalactites will be at it for eternity. Behind me, a throne to overthrow.

Maritime inlet. Big or little. Atlantic bonito. In the market, the same statues. The hairdresser erects a koutoubia in this street thrown together before Order. His hair peddled me stall to stall. Nothing more. I inquest. The star swings on its braid: tortured. How could one have sung it? Red-green! A hundred proverbs adopt it.

Africa is a veritable uniform. Gridirons. I unstick you. Light running against joy's grain. Agony and glory. In the thorn's empty heart, contiguity acclaims my eye. These are the silences, the grand syncopes. They nail polypteriformes to my spine wetter than the face of a prophet. Dawn slips out of my palms. Wait, no, I'm pulling my face out of the blackened grease.

a king sole jaundice a crypt
pistol alms lynching fake dollar
I disentomb the candid night from raw sand
fornicate lacerate my fugue and stray over the orgasm
of sour wines from compassless time where the forefinger
of the Bedouin crushes every coin and grudgelessly
polishes a star with your shadow which sinks in the abyss
when I carry your cadaver to the horoscopic register
of the stones of interrogation stitched with my laughter.

I have been to the disembowelings: GENNEVILLIERS. A devil leaps out of the fluted glass and cancels the xenophilic cloud my damage weaves. I put you in stitches. You will be a sluice in my rupture.

THEY ANNOUNCE
MY DEATH

this poster runs the fathomed air
breaks
but a break that only births
a discount king
not black and whose whip raises swastika striations
on the childhood walking in your cornea's cruel whiteness

he lives in a luxurious pigsty between shards of stars precocious thunder woodlice and fake businesses whose prayer ties categorical dictation to amber niches and carob trees that help it nullify itself this sun I juice whenever I'm thirsty under the medals incoming shells sacks of flour and the sugarloaves that comprise my only sex—I lean back into the onslaughts but I blow my top too soon knowing I have errands to run at the pinnacles of recent ruins in the authentic Dawn swollen with a musty whiff this the fiery hair of the daughter born of my desperation red pustule and a little blue She rolls her one bone over my back and flies away not too high but far enough away because I am looking for her and I see her completely blue red never white a little green rolling around on her shoulders hoarding her sparks the better with which to obliterate me.

At the edge of the city the ecstasy of my indifferences SUN AND TROUT tracked to a basin that literally loved me I collapsed inside a sharp laugh under the twigs with no other bird than my fatigue that was the song the swift quarrel of demise knelling the nearby sea a torrent flagged down before the water could reshuffle my identity LARGE PYRE FOR SINGLE MAN and who calls himself eclipse dead tongue DAY KILLED TAKEN SERIOUSLY according to

grandfather and his ancestor under threat of an accident overcome one never
knows how Beautiful smokescreens for avoiding the crosses like so many tones
flown to the landmarks that repeat me   me   this greasy spoon Sacking the
taste We have plugged the overexposed navel with a fist from the damaged
jimmied sky the coffers where you were hiding the unhappy eye of spring. It
attracted you addled you from afar where beside and even in me your sooty
silence rose in a mass of factory buildings and slums that mock the nest-eggs
slotted inside your tongues these our most serious brawls

nopal-land-pebble-land
and if my anus bucks and jumps
where the excellent germination of fantasy
plays its tarot cards
my urge harries and targets yes my burst
of work and stifled order
inspects your affairs in the Raffaello splendors
and the Bismarcks from which your shipwreck fires at me
the star seated in my kneecap.

A tilted childhood will strangle me. Pure! Toilet of horned vipers. The sand
lends its voice to the morning.

    THE SUN
    a swaybacked nag but I follow the trajectory
    between black flamingos and the newspaper
    of the steppes raised by police raiding
    the false incantations of laterites

I have an eye for twisting the inscriptions where you've planted me more than
sea spread over your ivory yacht subterfuges desert not stiff not yellow the
common midwife toads speak my divisions my oubliettes without which
death would be just another coffle I split through this eye bed down inside it

and replace you with a gust of rained-down blood get me vaccinated give me
the rain that refuses to fall

the gluttonous earth the yellow assegais of your piracy
nights of spasms and sarcasm
and days of slaps longer than the loose-lipped
sky but please acquit me of these masquerades
my wing describes the limit of
in which the prophet's vicissitudes are annulled
and not by the yew forgotten in my armpit
not by the water
of the burly adulterer rutting with a sex snipped
by the gardeners who carry my night

he hunted me but I always gave him the slip I could steal but couldn't vote the
Urn bloomed inside the sun like a squid delighted by what the sea brought
back to tempt the choreographed acrobatics and to bleed its chancre for this
cabal of men whose primary idiosyncrasy is to call itself people concrete neck-
ties newspaper wheelbarrow or lost bullet we didn't visit minarets or attics we
had other eyes these hands studied surreptitiously in the shadow of iotas con-
ceived by the beautiful ants of despair laughing morning and night all the way
up to the sour clouds who still haven't greeted the chergui of your salvations. I
had thrown my satchel in a wheelrut The city sank into itself Its electrism rang
out like coins dropped on a copper counter

I was the egg the boa the torture
of the talisman dismembered on my rind
weather coupled with rust-inducing words
making thrones that play
with my marbles and my pupils

my nose further such a grimace to take lightly It consumed me dislocated my ankles the elite fugitive slaves of my quarrels and I dredged it in black flour and sent it not to the cows but to the skittish chicks of my blood which it dared plug up with cowshit tineid moths and gravel pored over I don't know how many times by the sumptuous poets driven back to the edge of the abyss I demolished the temples burned the archives of the world and started the Negative Man running They saw him pass by like a flaming hoop among freshly trimmed beards seasonal garb and public affairs They thought him fairy bankruptcy panicked angel but they were mistaken since I had closed all the museums the mosques the churches and the factories where the Word was no longer valid but as soon as I saw again a meadow a bird a tree flowering or not I called in winter had it immediately refine the land so I could sculpt on it a white house from the black page of time then quietly walk the wild laughter I wrested from the men mid-dream mid-beating in the fundamental alleyway where you steered me wrong starting with school and even after you tore out my seams

Hirsute. Bilious cow. Salads. Articulations, but this weak sex skids towards the beltway of moldy cities. No, Madame Shrimp. Vertebra and salt. This is the plate. She's doing much better this morning. Carats for a night of goodnatured ribbing. Greens as is. The little gossips. The old porpoises. The lizards my hearing vaccinates. Voyeur, you confer on me a marsupializing virtue. He comes to us from well-behaved stars. Me, the Scented Juice? Don't pistol that. Pop your doctored wine that I decreed to whoever'd listen. He leaves so much my belly ached and then let's never speak of it again. The old crow who took its teeth from the crocodile poor crocodile. He's playing the soldier of a poorly excavated culture. Not watered by our suns. Not sparklingly at any rate. I wouldn't know you from my asshole except I did see you once among the hazy gray of my amazements. He left at word one. IN THIS OLD CHAOS OF LETTERS DAMNED AND DAMNED AGAIN WHAT TO MAKE OF THE ERA OF LITTLE ELITES WHO DOZE ON THE PINK LAUREL ABUSED INTO YELLOW? He's coming back in two days, I want the heads of every pin, I want your narcotic shit. No shit, nothing holy! I'm going to dress you good man, you only have to let yourself be measured. I turn the dogma, I'm going spinal. Whup, half-pint without winter, the foam, it roots in me so perfectly. But I don't like the high places, the guts wherein my and the one true god's poop slosh and intermix with ease. Every ten minutes I go to the potty. I won't sell myself piece by piece into the hole. I practice, you know how… the AGONY about which no one ever dares say a word. That's awful, hush up. No I can't anymore. I won't gobble up your advice. Here is my produce, but rhythms rare and fearless, totally vulgar; my tapestries of pitchforks more grimacing than grimaced at; open like the mouth of a puppy who never got its big teeth. They won't throw me this bone, Mr. Dapper. They avoid me so I shouted… Or better yet throw it down the hole and never mind.

Such assholes these little conductors of inedible algae!
Do you agree blood-paul-crumb while you chew with me
on these involucres stuffed with the stars of false flags?
The colossal inquest keeps digging.

the CALUMET is not of my design
I make leashes to walk the real suns with
I electric and do not promise
a night an empty season an eyelash add up to nothing
everything yelled just to be said
repeated committed committing
with the black sacraments of the desert that hustles
closer every second

The flag can no longer be drunk! The legend is repulsive!
We are the Newly Dead!

this rose garden where the night disturbs me doesn't satisfy my thirst
jumping ounces wasted malice
teeth not rotted but chipped by sour wines

every night
when I press to my forehead the nude of gutted grottos
a sheet of blotter paper dries me out haunts me
has me taste the salt of words
talking
to almost no one except for those soaking
in the discounted pure blood of a rhacophorus sun

Manifesto

extorted and chewing on ink   I
she's aged cut dried on top of her child
and the exquisite sun in which her structure falters   l
I wrest loose my old sprains   o
carve the slum into its pitted fruit   s
this void she multiplied by herself   e

                                               n
                                               o
                                               t

not a bone not a belt not even close so I reel
between my chastened wings

but she was getting hard to recognize
she spit her face around me
saying writing without principle
what I don't know me a scattered mule
and we buck ourselves off
if only it were about taking seriously the truth
camouflaged
under hems green and sometimes smoldering
I would have stood myself at the bottom of its zipper
I would work at it and not without irking
the screw that alters my words!

In the fields of agaves and young nopals where the light describes the trajectory of truths extinguished, there is a skin of shadow and putrid mud that leads the sky to the tapered end of a modern conflict without it ever resulting in a space other than that of a black-on-gray-blue tragedy. But didn't it rearrange in its brain a hole for murder? Everything began with a dream (true or false), everything was ready to be put in play but nothing jockeyed to the front of the line that wasn't what fidgeted inside me spurting irregularly but in an electric and charming manner. As no gaze ever settled upon it, it was burned vertically so no one could guess that all along the entire composition was supported by nothing but a string of lives wasted in advance!

The theater that is going to enact itself must thus be made of movable words and particles and can have nothing emotional about it if the movement is to animate it organically and drive it gradually passion being only one of the multiple residues of the childishness of expressed forms and the elaboration of the drama via transgressive gestures and impulsions which engage it on a flat surface where it gathers value from the nominal act. From the outset everything is theater, even the tiniest writing, even a judicial deposition. But in a similar case, the real and the realistic blend together and organize themselves in such a unity that it is with ease one can classify their antagonisms and return to a geophysical discipline which would surpass the stadium of the simple theory of structures or the study of stratification.

If it is right and true that the written theater is not without a fundamental participation by the human depoeticized at the time of its implementation, the lesson within it is so obvious that the poem thus sketched (schematically the theater) enters my skin and wears it down expanding its substance towards infinity until it erodes my skin completely. My skin thus becomes theater itself. This explains the fact that an actor or a simple speaker may be moved by pulsations whose original significations he might ignore. My skin unlearns itself in order to disintegrate while at the same time it reconstitutes itself in a language whose words are separated from their ordinary phraseological texture to which the eyes surrender at first sight and which the ear translates by a necessary association with events to come.

We learn then that the theater is textual and inscribes itself in an order neither metaphoric nor lyric—even when one speaks of the most inflammatory writing—but put simply the continuation of a clean idea, of theater founded principally on the movement and frequency of the word conquered as soon as one opposes the static principle of its recognized originality or the other principles in which is displayed a superlative precarity and which discomfit and dishonor before provoking the very idea of the word.

Land! Up to now still named red and even blue emptied by a howl. Not life. Something other than silence.

THE FIRST TO ARRIVE

Whether I am black gray blue doesn't matter now things are turning towards the good as if it were me speaking no I grasp nothing having nothing more to force me inside my head I lost not the meaning of crumbs of events of hours it doesn't count anymore first of my losses is myself first to arrive first to be lost for you who are behind this speaker for I don't know how many crossings-over-to-death and other insignificant sequences. I am my true father!

THE QUESTIONER

Go on!

THE FIRST TO ARRIVE

Everything in due time, good sir! Even an injury Which only heats itself as much as the other who is neither more nor less than a cadaver!

I batter papa.

I pocket his sardines,
the lenses he doesn't wear, his sleep.

The rosary
The woman

                                      Africa
in its entirety hears this riddled with bullets
I made from Lumumba a bloody old flag
Africa hoists his death to the height of diplomatic silences
in horror it saws the bill and the masks in which God
sits among the garbage dumps
and the numbers that no longer intimidate me

                              THE WARRIOR FOUGHT ALL
NIGHT AGAINST HIMSELF ALONE
DEATH LEAKS FROM OUR IRREPLACABLE MIDWIFE TOADS
HE MADE HIMSELF A PRISON OF ASH AND A CEMETERY FOR HIM
        ALONE
ON OUR COMPROMISED FACES THERE IS
A PEOPLE WHO SURVIVE ON SCARS
A TRUE SCHOLAR FORNICATES IN A BASE
MENT

your proud snout took me between quotes
counted quanta the steel bands of the boat sunk
into
the eye
shitty dromedary rotten
this guy used in an episode
of God the Anarch!

                      And so my mother was beaten with a pole
on her buttocks her head her vagina whimpering her name knowing
her dentition corroborated my excuses
o papa monstrous millionaire thank you for knowing yourself

so little
she opened herself like a legitimate chancre
without a father I
would have been thrown in a well
to exonerate the scrubbed
irradiating reflecting wetly on my berber
syllables
and my wife young and popping a thousand weather balloons
I will shove you in the oven with the other hells (get it?)
putrescent climate
president to my conception of the world And what my father
wanted   for
ME
it's essential
to have disconnected two asses knowing that my thing
is essential
and that the sperm I am and ejaculate now and then
is a perfect realization of my cantankerous character
under the forest its terrors its termited terrain its
sieves and
floods
the respite waits for a new ounce to explode
and give reason to the bipedal-basket-of-dried-figs
to my insolent men
Tell me everything blue blood
novel out of story a life out of print
in the holes which are nothing less than the un
theatrical theater a fugue of blood crusting the lips
of dusty books
resting on a heap of mellow shit A CARICATURE OF
LIFE SOCIALLY DIFFERENTIATED
though it is precisely life that decapitates with laughter

fat and empty swell and plump WITHOUT GUTTURAL SCREAMS
NOTHING
LESS!

The word is thus the fact of an ancient intoxication
the word is thus the fact of a naked toad boasting
the word is thus fashioned and is nobody's not even the scholars
hypothesized and candied the shrewd ones whom I notice
on my beach
nobody's
not even this human flowerbed's
not even the man-of-cuttlefish-bones's who my birds and the cyclopes
tacked onto the wall
detect inside my barracks
...
I am a train of spies a pigsty a shepherd's crook
behind me time makes sense
dorsal fin
shark that I am
shark that I'll stay

                              they sent wusfi to the moon
they sent Hache on a long walk
                     they sent Ker to Cairo No damage Moscow's watch-
ing The canal is a buckler The pyramids? A millenary obstacle, let us reap the
wheat of Islam! It's asking questions about the tanks and undelivered mirages
It starts in on a crappy story and patches its eye of terrible auguries They sent
me off to more easily mutilate me

in a schoolboy's notebook *I* poisoned the language of things they rectified my
past saying It's too bad you're bigger than this Blessed be the illusion which
pushes us to the point of attributing to the role that hurries us away toward a

rattapallax fate a correction of the facts that won't occur without souring us
They mount the revolt They chopped up the universal which is to say local
suffrage The world thus obliterated life which is the land the land which is the
sky and the ocean which is a vast vat of sperm blessedly strong all add up to
only one!

NO LONGER DO I SEE MY BLOOD THROUGH THE PRISM OF THE
VIRTUAL GODS WHO ONCE FASCINATED ME TRANSLATED ME
INTO NUMBERS AND RUMBLED IN MY SALACIOUS EXHAUSTIONS
SHARPENING THE EDGE OF MY HATREDS BUT I DISCERN IN
MAN A PATH WHICH BRINGS HIS CHAIN OF TREASONS PAST
WINTER WHERE SNOW DELIVERED ITS INSULTS TO THE SUN
SURROUNDING IT AND HARRYING IT INTO THE SONG WE
LIMPIDLY STRIKE UP WHEN THE HYENA-MOUTHED MAN BEGAN
WRITING THE TEXT THAT WOULD UNDO HIM

a talky old harridan turns up and says to me
This is your name the media is so out of it but they always manage (the carni-
vores) to put their thumb in their ass and their eye to an ear
if you want to talk familiarly that's just fine
these awful times won't end without it The dead king oh what will we do with
the republics still patronized by dialectical colonialism and the come-and-go
of my hide bled to white by the blackmailers the plantation owners of South-
North-America The appointed cancer of South Africa They still refund me a
little of the money owed: their
sure But Vietnam's no cancer it's an imperialist tidal wave of Yahoos as Swift
would call them! I'm organizing famine in the hearths of Africa
who roaming adobe error
juggle the splendor of thunder from a country
larger
than all the Americas united
which includes of course the u

rine striped with the blood
of communities cervically established to under
stand Communist Asia
the USSR and this Africa not at all African When
will that be?

Trees slid across the ineffable—real tunnel or brothel. This is the procedure for
lights alive in infertile times. Here is the city opening with a tintinnabulation
of rootless ouds! On the summit where madness watches its left flank, it
invents a molecular God. It drives us mad, being the scar of unreality and
urgent words yelled out. Charred as we are! We rise up under this skin and
dare to recognize ourselves in the fetishes night undressed. Having heard it all
and understood it my birds collapse. Dog-drawn carriage! This change isn't
worth a cent. You won't get me to swallow this gold. You will shrivel this statue
however heavy your rumen and me annulled by every sacrifice. The play
begins where shrewdness ends.

                                they pacified me
swimming between them better than kelp roaches
between them and me I was swimming superbly better than
THE ENORMOUS RACKET UNDER A SIMPLE SHAME
being at once both poorly built and mightily stiff
authorizing
the rest of the most rancid literature! What crap!
AN X FLEW BY CUTTING UP RECONSTITUTED TROYS
balls made a heap which pulverized them Oh my bible!
by the sacramental qur'an and by all its murderers
swore the autochthonous god to the frozen blood!

I have closed all the books and opened only my memory
they told me a word needs but one man
living on the rail of intangible paths and bedrooms

with any genitals except this repugnant unpayable
frugality
of beings worked over by codes
they made it so my voice couldn't be more than thunder
waving its pizzle over the dead city
of blood spurting rebuking even the light
the fief the phlegm leaking from the sinister prevaricator
and silent while they adjust my nose
and my hearing
my balls were scraping against the sky flowing above as over
the continent's most incontestable waterfalls and the
warriors were coming with difficulty to the world monopolized
by calamitous camaraderies which kill it
grain after grain
coition after flagellation It drank black
straps and reflected Thought and man remembering
his
stature
It became a gigantic rotary
of morose colors and reflections of
atomized bees!

                    trembling tamadount
                    prayer and disease!
canceled cuckolds of load-bearing taxes
of our names and of sap given here
to the ruptures so they'll tear out the seams with testicular trances!

          the freak spits on
himself

          green
the feast

settle up finish the guinea pigs
we sing we dance we rhyme we trance we yell we i
odine on the im
manence
at the edge of the sea in the light of the dunes in a joyous circle the boat
which outdoes me unhorns me pokes me in the eye this business
is
largely feral

                                a

                        you have

blowfishes

                nebulously

o

                        offsquared

                        I'm a winner every minute but space
which opened itself no longer needs this pocket change
exchange is a final offer of oneself to the insects
which certify adapt my accusatory legend
I saw the Earth denting the sky the martian lickspittle
who at once deserves and damns my fear
this is the devil invented by the blackmailers of souls
graying
at the zero hour
they work in the gayest peat bogs
they entrance the knack and the man

ear of a woman as of a kite
of society as of a nightmare
of God as of some entity criminally priced
of me as of a zero rising from below while simultaneously
from the high plateau of sorrows taken seriously
they tidy anger into fires propitiating the solar globe
and nothing will be left except moldy ideas dates and
bluish convolutions ravaged by antibiotics
which Pasteur and the strangler shepherd of clumsy
suspicion
discovered and never invented
on the cold void of a window!
                              This is the spot where the bank notes de
tour   into rubles   into agaves   but
never to emaciated biafrans   Egypt wages war
elsewhere
holy pilots the egyptians?
go on
root rotting in the null skin of a jailed Jew
a SIX DAY cage this daily newspaper pops the faith
in numbers
the great composer of concupiscent homilies is
DEAD!

mine are the transoms of the un-civil prison
mine the anarchy mine the Ford Taunus loose stones
of cobalt
the nabobs
the kings I kill incidentally with the workings of my machine
in
where
over

94

by
with
without
which well fuck me But the big smokescreen is a King
shitting paths making
cream for this people
unsought by stiff plagues and uncalled
by the bells of the
unorganized
cadaverized
meal restored to the original corruption of the first orgasm
struck midflight with rust because no right ever had
a single woman
aside from the grasshopper and the teenage bandit to split open
and it caresses them harmfully between two glasses forgotten
on the bar
aside from its rump red as a shameful nightcrawler
aside from some thing (maybe a carafe of hot water)
that sings
balloons
gargles and gags its existence with I-do-it-my-way-or-
not-
at-all!

                silhouette pardon and rudiments
dog this myself happily
I make the clouds I despise the rain the Negev is mine
spat onto my aerial phallus like the old mirage
of Dassault
that sodomizes Concorde solemnly
ass with which old senility's ablutions builds a palace
over brothel

all are like the fleas gobbling up the miserable france!
that's right!
no capital f for france!
have at it my hairy brothers my argan-loving centipedes
ferociously the tribe in an explosion of fistulas
and asthma

                    But
smackdab in the middle of Paris THEY KILLED BEN BARKA AND
HASSAN II PUT
ANOTHER IN HIM
But
what's the party care oh screw the gangrenous old party!
He doesn't kill he pays Oufkir to kill with
a puff of smoke
no one here smokes hash
everyone drops LSD. It's *de rigeur*, non?
We
pistolwhipped the King
he laughed at our stunningly serious quirks
we
deboned
the King
who mocked in the air our scientific quagmire
and
our grammars
and our
mothers complicit as the land
we
rebuked Oufkir
All of that is dead
I kill the outhouse day

I am mad I slam on the ground kings presidents and
syndicates of dismembered locomotives complicit as
the baaing of frozen sheep
syndicate mother
president father turbulent king
go incinerate your fucking diaphragm!
straightaway a hard-on!
swordlessly I kill the king my machine's an atom bomb
better not
use it against the palace morocco might burst completely
into flame thank you Seddik royally appointed hobo old
two face!

my pen could be not just its weight but an asthmatic rifle,
a fellagha's rifle!
I assemble it in a single motion which has never been
seen before
and has neither name nor qualifier
to defend the primordial rights of the chancellor
limping
a hut my apple out of which Adam steps
cinematographically
his head cracks open in the desert of my desertude
he gives birth to an unleashable echo
in order to build his fall with an ordinary ellipse
when the city assembles my gut
launches an asteroid at me
and tells me Freud the implacable snow of support
and Marx a febrile surgeon
and thunderously myself the others teeming inside
coughing morbidly in the arch
of the cemetery of putrefying whales

these are the things that batter and harry my nights
the creak of the hinges of this terrorist terrain
these are the cries of children thrown in the garbage
of the cache of weapons unsold
to kuwaits rutilant in medieval shit!
earth fissured
begrudging
icy breast and curdled mother's milk
I abhor black gold but I obey
I kill the bloodless king the king is not even the dog
who smuggles me across the plains of this true dream!

I write against
this is the negative man
my father
beaten into retirement in his
country home
and having
my mother beaten by an unknown carrier of rustic lamps
and bowls of experimental hemlock which we
remember
at the slightest suggestion

the other who overtakes Me
        his mother spits out
her heterogeneous heart She
scribbles stiffly on
his EYE   But
the nomads will always listen to the refineries
of petrol and
the devaluations
they're mine I tell you the supreme thistle and twitch grass

tricolor!
mine are the ravenous hyenas who season my coffin
stripping it only of lust and ascending nails
who act like the gods of ill-fitting keys
and build out of their genitals a hangar of scoundrels
he's mine
THE DEAD KING

Now and forever!

Notes

ascomycete – a member of the fungal phylum *Ascomycota*, which includes molds, mildews, and yeasts, truffles, and morels.

assegai – an iron-tipped spear.

Bandung – a reference to the Afro-Asian Conference held in Bandung, Indonesia, in 1955, to promote economic cooperation and resistance to colonialism among Global South nations.

Bou Regreg – a river that begins in the Middle Atlas Mountains, runs past the capital of Rabat, and ends in the Atlantic Ocean.

chergui – a hot dry wind that blows easterly and southeasterly in Morocco out of the Sahara Desert.

Draa – the longest river in Morocco, which runs westward through the center of the country.

elytrons – the hard forewings of a beetle that protectively cover the functional wings.

fellagha – Arabic for bandits; also, term used to identify anti-colonial fighters in the Algerian War of Independence (1954–62).

forficulid – a type of earwig.

Gennevilliers – an outlying suburb (*banlieue*) of Paris. Unlike suburbs in the U.S., where the affluent tend to cluster, Parisian suburbs tend to be lower income. These suburbs can function almost like ghettos to which immigrant and minority populations have been consigned.

gymnodactyl – resembling a gecko, in particular a genus of gecko found in Brazil and commonly called naked-toe geckoes.

hemipter – an insect in the order *hemiptera*, also known as "true bugs." This order contains a wide variety of insects, such as aphids and cicadas. Hemipters can reproduce via parthenogenesis, or the production of offspring from unfertilized eggs.

Ifni – a small former Spanish colony located within French Morocco, which was formally returned to Morocco in 1969.

involucre – the protective, specially developed, typically short leaves that undergird the petals of a flower.

julid – a millipede from the order *julidae*.

Koutoubia – the largest mosque in Marrakesh.

laterites – a soil and rock type that is red due to a high iron oxide content and which occurs mostly in the tropics. It is the result of laterization, or tropical weathering, which replaces soluble substances that occur naturally in the rock with insoluble ones.

lithobe – a centipede in the genus *lithobius*, commonly known as stone centipedes and which are found under stones and in decaying matter.

mygalomorph – a spider belonging to the infraorder *mygalomorphae*, which includes tarantulas, mouse spiders, trapdoor spiders, and other large, straight-fanged spiders.

myriapoda – a subphylum of arthropods which includes millipedes, centipedes, and other similar, many-legged insects.

polypteriform – a fish belonging to an order of ray-finned fish native to the Nile, preferring swampy and shallow habitats; also known as a bichir.

Translator's Afterword

Mohammed Khaïr-Eddine died on Moroccan independence day in 1995 and is buried in the capital, Rabat. We may only have his words today, but it's important to remember that they once emerged from his body.

Khaïr-Eddine was Amazigh, part of the ethnic group (also known as Berber) that has lived in Morocco for millennia. Over the course of those millennia, outside empires—Phoenician, Roman, Arab, French—have "pacified," parceled, exchanged, pillaged, and retreated from this land, all the while regarding his and his peoples' bodies as inconvenient obstacles to their imperial aspirations. In fact, the Imazighen, who make up about 40 percent of the Moroccan population, remain so inconvenient that only as recently as 2005 was their language (Tamazight) allowed to be taught in schools; only in 2011 was the language recognized officially in Morocco's constitution. This feeling of inconvenience, of being a barrier to overcome or object to remove, drives Khaïr-Eddine's work and his awareness of the political and biological complexities of the body. He strives to reclaim, as Yusef Komunyakaa calls it, "this space / my body believes in." In the opening poem of this collection, "Black Nausea," Khaïr-Eddine begins by placing inside himself the true inconvenience—namely, the lies the conquerors have spread to make their conquest easier: that his home is a wasteland, rumored to have once been inhabited, but now abandoned. Khaïr-Eddine digests the lies, using their dubious nutrition to fuel vociferous refutations that point to his and his people's bodies and the positions they've been crammed into: decomposing, wandering, spitting, living on the margins and in exile, vomiting, attacking, assembling.

Over the course of his life, Khaïr-Eddine wrote more than a dozen books, ostensibly divided into several collections of poetry and several novels, though he found the border drawn between genres anathema. As seen in this collection, in poems like "Gennevilliers" and "Scorpionic Sun," Khaïr-Eddine blends modes without hesitation. He found most borders anathema. Divisions between self and other, art and politics, one ethnic group or language and another, were tools of division, the fruits of "a Europe under the illusion that it possessed universal truths and values that could be applied to all peoples" and which, along with "military supremacy[,] technology [and] Western science colonized [the Maghreb]," in the words of fellow poet Abdellatif Laâbi (62). This refusal of arbitrary, imperially mandated and violently enforced borders undergirds his work. It also inaugurated *Souffles*, an avant-garde literary journal he assisted Laâbi, Mostafa Nissaboury, and other Moroccan intellectuals of the '60s in founding and producing. The journal broke new ground in the North African arts scene for many reasons, but one of the most significant was its position on language. Though many at the time were advocating for exclusive use of Arabic, as a rebuke to the French, Laâbi et al. asserted that French was just as legitimate and important a language with which to revolutionize postcolonial artistic expression. By forbidding French—the language of politics and education in Morocco—the pro-Arabic faction was likely forcing many writers and intellectuals to express themselves in a less familiar language. As Laâbi says in "Réalités et dilemmes de la culture nationale," "[y]ou do not betray your people by glorifying its struggle, whatever the means" (68).

Souffles, like Khaïr-Eddine, advocated for a radical, leftist, large-tent approach to art, politics, and culture. It is perhaps unsurprising that this threatened the dominant political order to the extent that Khaïr-Eddine went into exile in France in the late '60s. In the early '70s, *Souffles* was shuttered and Laâbi as its editor in chief was imprisoned for "crimes of opinion." Many of the poems in this collection take aim at the source of this 'order,' King Hassan II, whose 30-plus-year reign is known as "the years of lead" due to his consistent, brutal, paranoiac repression of dissent. The paranoia wasn't entirely baseless: in 1972, General Mohamed Oufkir, the king's right-hand man (mentioned twice in "Manifesto"), conspired to have Hassan II's airliner shot down (by the Moroccan Air Force, no less). The attempt failed, and the king had Oufkir executed and his family confined to a remote desert prison for more than a decade. This wasn't Oufkir's first assassination attempt: he was also the architect of multiple operations against Mehdi Ben Barka, a prominent opposition politician to whom "Description of a Flag" is dedicated. Ben Barka, similar to Khaïr-Eddine, was forced into exile for his commitment to getting Morocco to value the lives, livelihoods, and contributions of all of its subjects. He was internationally renowned: he met with Che Guevara and Malcolm X during his exile, and was in charge of the planning committee for the Tricontinental Conference in Havana in 1966. Ben Barka never attended: he disappeared in Paris in 1965, thanks to Oufkir's orchestrations. His body was never found.

When I first encountered Khaïr-Eddine's work, in Pierre Joris and Habib Tengour's *Poems for the Millennium, Volume 4*, an anthology of North African literature from 2013, I was amazed by how he brings together bodies separated by enormous swathes of experience, time, and space. The poems are aware of themselves as bodily phenomena, artifacts that emerge from and recompose themselves in a body. Via his attention to sound, his pastiche of cadences, his use of shock and disgust and indignation, and other poetic armaments, he brings his reader into a renewed consciousness of the body, its quirks and spurts, its limits and infinities, its feelings of being a spatiotemporal burden and miracle. It is with these arms that Khaïr-Eddine wages his "linguistic guerilla war" on the French language, a term he used to describe his indefatigable, improvisatory, erudite assaults on the language used to erase his and others' experiences so that he can then reconstitute it to communicate these experiences.

My translation aims to preserve or reproduce the poems' bodily effects so we don't forget the work emerges from a body occupying contested space and time. Most frequently, this sense of embodiment manifests itself in Khaïr-Eddine's use of sound. Perhaps the most prominent example is the title. Where Khaïr-Eddine used *Soleil arachnide*, which translates literally to *Spider Sun*, I've gone with *Scorpionic* instead. Why? In order to reproduce, I hope, in the mouth and the ear, the sonic traffic jam of the original. "Spider sun" lacks the contrast of the smooth *soleil* (soh-layə) with the throaty growl of *arachnide* (ah-rakh-need). "Scorpionic sun" inverts the sonic progression, and doesn't offer as noticeable or aggressive a contrast, but does play *r* and hard-*c* sounds off the benign-sounding sibilance and nasality of *sun*, approximating some of the sonic friction, if not shock, of the original—which itself intimates the collection's mashup of the elegant and the visceral. Elsewhere in the text where I've changed up word choice or order, it's for this same reason: to approximate a sequence of sounds and the argument it makes inside the mouth, throat, and ear.

The title is one of the few overt liberties I've taken with Khaïr-Eddine's very precise use of scientific terms. (In my defense, scorpions are an order in the arachnid class, so it's more of a particularization than an outright substitution.) Throughout the book, Khaïr-Eddine employs a variety of hyper-specific, esoteric terms: words like laterites (a type of reddish clay), elytron (the parts of a beetle's shell sheathing the wings), and julid (a type of millipede), which evoke various natural phenomena and species. I have preserved these as much as possible throughout, since they betray an important attention to the life around him and the language needed to evoke it in its fineness, while also jolting the reader. By packaging familiar plants and objects in the form-fitting linguistic film of Latinate taxonomy, Khaïr-Eddine shows the distance that language can put between us and the world we use it to describe. Instead of seeing reddish stone, or the corrugated iridescence of a beetle's shell, we see the smooth unyielding surface of the word, before we look it up, move our eyes off the world and into the systems of knowledge others have promulgated about it.

He's also signaling to us that he, a postcolonial subject, can deploy the recondite, remote language of Western scientific discourse with ease. Diction is a kind of discursive posture, after all, a way for a speaker to signal their membership in particular groups, a means of providing a proper code so the body can move freely. And Khaïr-Eddine adopts a lot of postures, moving swiftly between skulk and march and prostration, asserting his right to exist in certain spaces. This swiftness gives his poetry its athletic, almost spastic, vigor. His use of slang is essential to this repertoire. His desire to exploit the metaphorical aspects of the slang, though, can present some difficulties in translation. For instance, he ends "Memorandum" with the idiom "froid aux yeux," which literally means "cold-eyed," but in the vernacular means, more or less, to quail, lose heart, freeze up. In the context of this poem, the phrase also redeploys components of an earlier image—"l'esclave aux yeux gelés"—namely, eyes and cold. Khaïr-Eddine is using this connection between the flute-playing slave and the symbolically violent and empowering word *pistol* to encourage us to consider further connections between these two. If I were to use the English idiom "cold feet" (my first choice) in the last line, I'd only half-approximate the connection. We'd get the cold, but not the eyes, and we'd lose the connection to the slave mentioned above since cold is an ephemeral quality not an innate feature. So, I decided to go with "does not blink," to emphasize the eyes and make the connection more evident. This gets rid of cold, risking that the connection isn't evident enough, but at least we've associated the bodily features of both moments, while preserving the gesture toward the demotic on which Khaïr-Eddine ends the poem so forcefully and menacingly.

Not every idiomatic usage comes with such intricately woven baggage—in the title poem, for instance, the rapid-fire poly-vocal passages of overheard slang seem included more for texture and volume than for their ability to point out language's in-built capacity for violence and denigration. But Khaïr-Eddine enjoys puns and extended metaphors throughout, and sometimes his linguistic inventiveness is more clever than I am and forces me to make a clean choice between the idiom and a more literal translation. In those cases, I err toward the literal (often more surreal) option, in order to preserve the strange, discomfiting image of, say, a gas-beaked diaphanously winged pigeon instead of a gaslight (*bec à gaz*). The ambiguity of the pun may be lost, but the defamiliarizing result of the attention that Khaïr-Eddine brings to the idiom is, I hope, partially preserved—the reader re-sees the idiom as a strange residue of cultural metaphor, and considers then what else in language is obscured.

Defamiliarization is, ultimately, Khaïr-Eddine's most prominent tool and sensation. He employs it to, as Abdellatif Laâbi puts it, "disarticulate his language, do violence to it, in order to extract all its possibilities." The choices I've made in this translation aim to conjure the feelings of vigor and strangeness beating inside his poetry. Khaïr-Eddine wrings sound, sensation, and shock out of the French language as he contorts it—so it sees, describes, laments, reviles, and praises the bodies it has been used to erase. If nothing else, I hope that my attempts here prompt others to engage with this writer of titanic, discomfiting talents. Today, as more anti-democratic politicians gain power by debasing language, dividing communities, silencing the marginalized, and flattening diversity into a cudgel, Khaïr-Eddine's work—and the furious pitch at which he delivers it—is indispensable.

Works Cited

Laâbi, Abdellatif. "Realities and Dilemmas of National Culture." Translated by Olivia C. Harrison and Teresa Villa-Ignacio. In *Souffles-Anfas: A Critical Anthology from the Moroccan Journal of Culture and Politics*, edited by Olivia C. Harrison and Teresa Villa-Ignacio. 61–73. Stanford: Stanford University Press, 2016.

Acknowledgments

Sincere gratitude is offered to the following journals, in which the following poems first appeared:

BOMB Magazine	"Where," "Barrage," "Laterites"
Nashville Review	"To White," "Refusing Burial"
Poetry Northwest	"Sagho," "Horoscope," "To Jean Dufoir"
Waxwing	"Barbarian," "Swashbuckling," "Exile"

I would also like to thank Pierre Joris, for his help in finding and contextualizing the work; Sam Ross, for fielding my importunate inquiries; and Travis Webster, for his encouragement and generous, vigorous support.

Thanks to Jennifer Grotz, the Katherine Bakeless Nason Endowment, and everyone at the Bread Loaf Translators' Conference for making it possible for me to attend and receive crucial feedback, and thanks to my workshop-mates for their thoughtful readings of earlier drafts. Thanks to Mónica de la Torre, Andrew Bourne, Bill Carty, Rajiv Mohabir, and Samuel Rutter, for wanting to see these poems in the world as much as I do.

Thanks to Jamie Ferguson, Anthony Abiragi, Valerie Howell, and all my teachers (en particulier ceux du Lycée Henri Matisse), for the examples of their patience, wisdom, and care; to my parents, for pushing me to move beyond so many borders; and to Rachel, for coming with me, and reeling me back in.

Finally, enormous gratitude to Hilary Plum, Caryl Pagel, and everyone at the Cleveland State University Poetry Center—for fishing this from the open call; for the meetings and phone calls and guidance and advice; for being such careful and caring stewards of this version of Khaïr-Eddine's vision.